Biff and Chip had a cookbook.

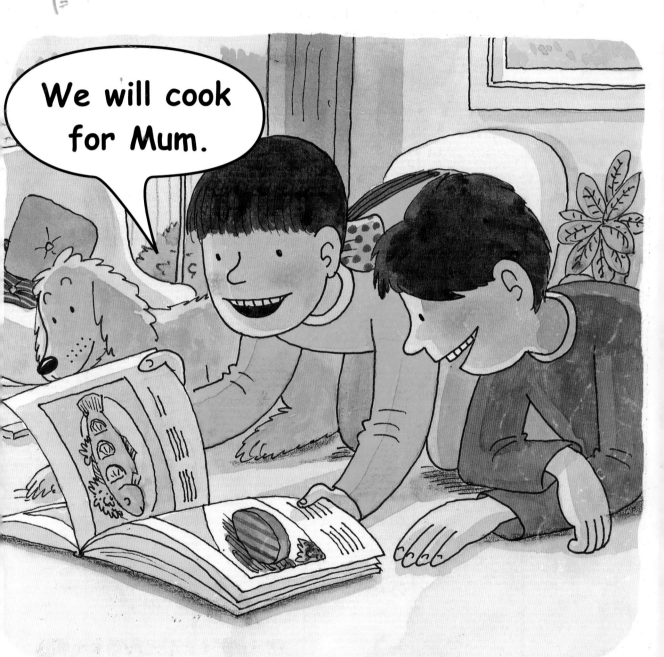

They had lots of leeks.

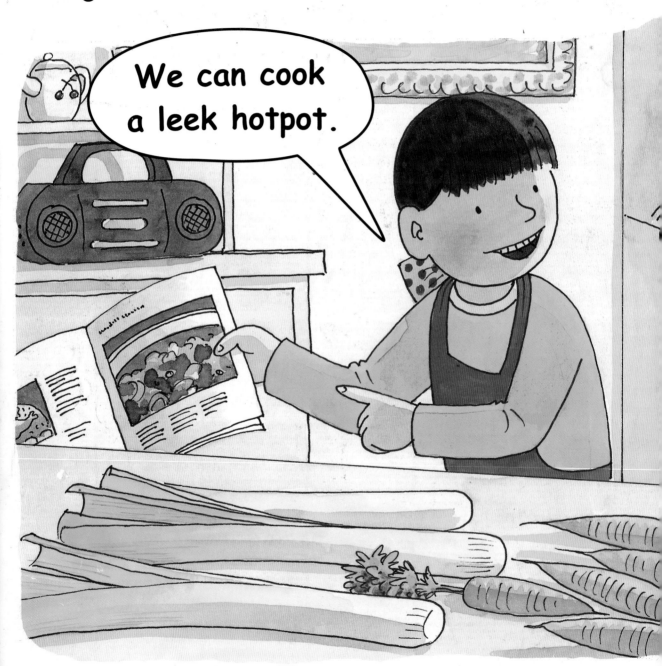

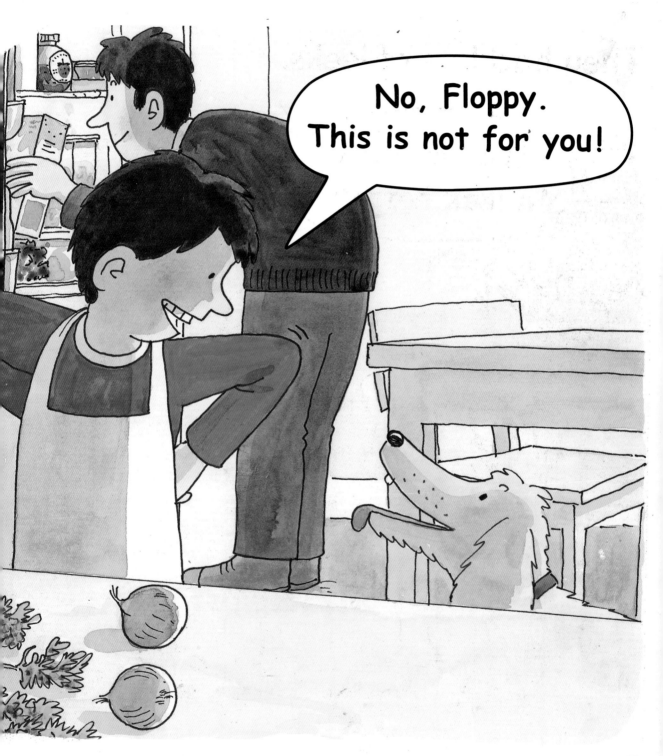

3

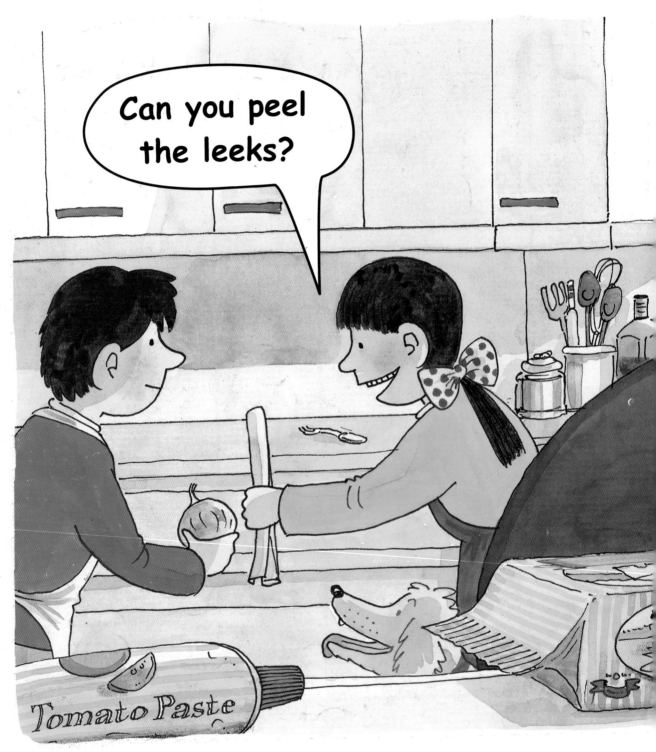

4

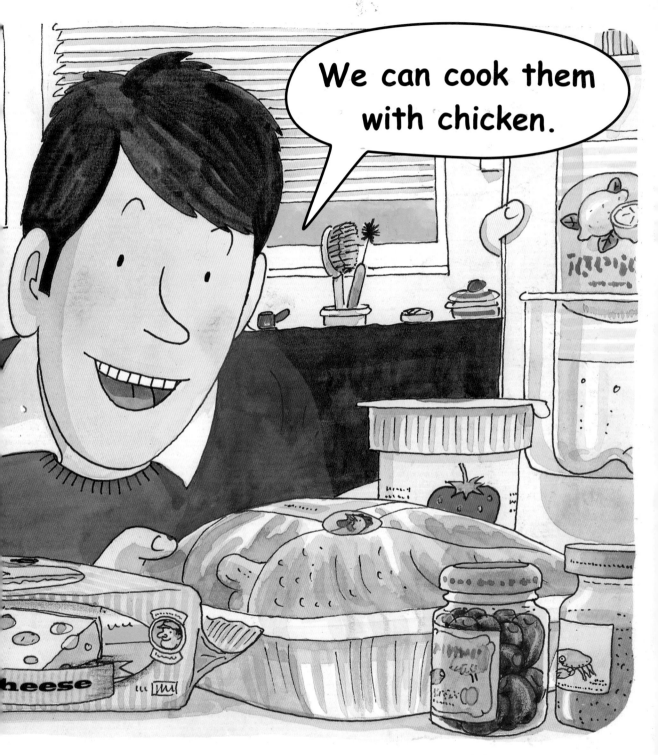

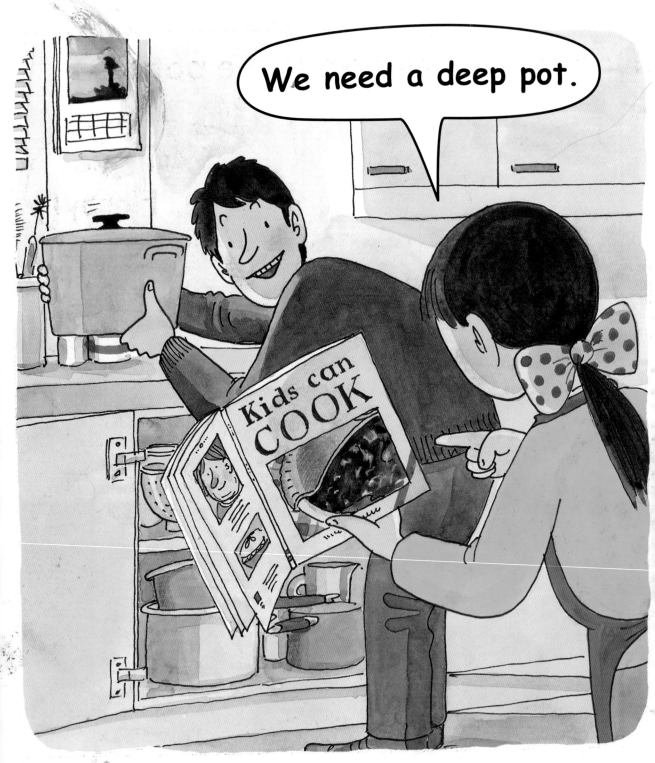

Dad put the chicken in the pot.

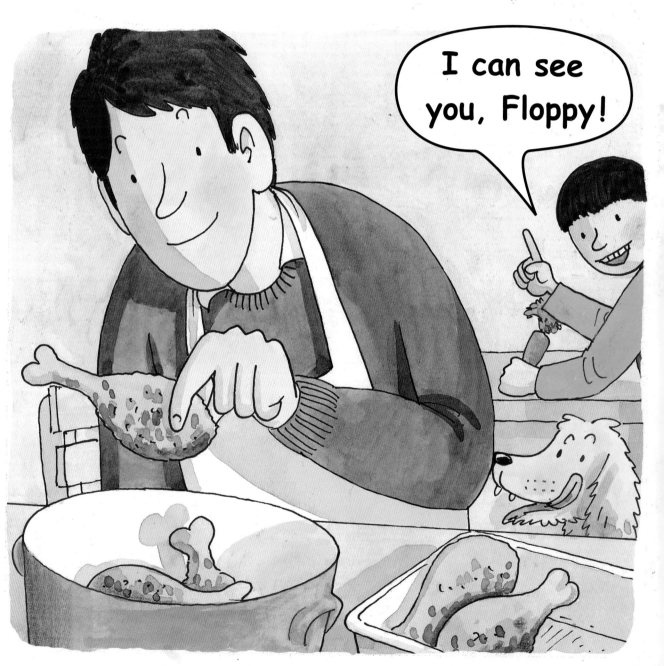

Biff put in the leeks.

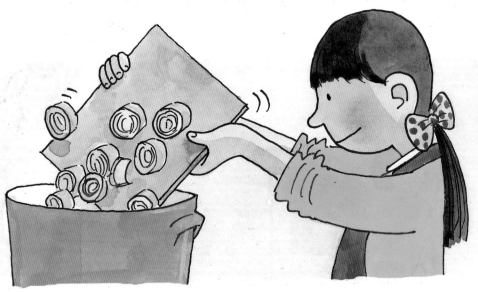

Then Dad put the pot on the hob.

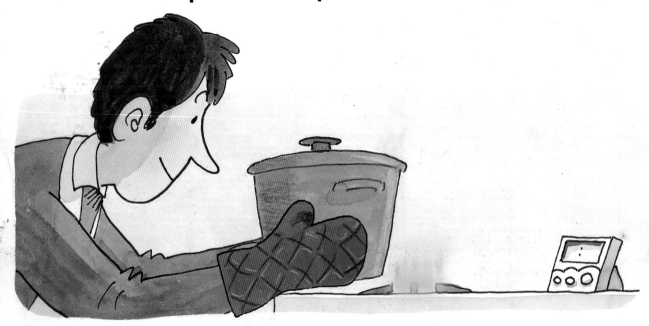

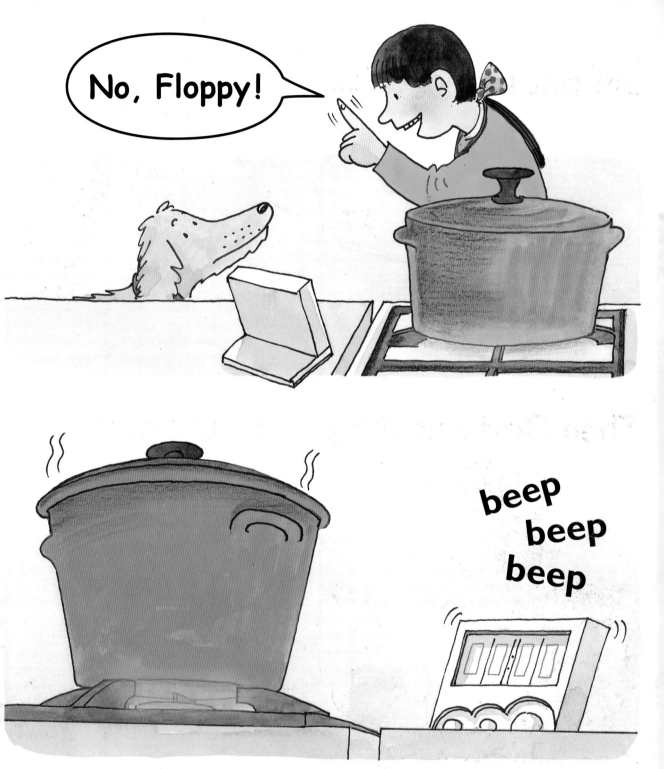

9

Dad took the lid off the hotpot.

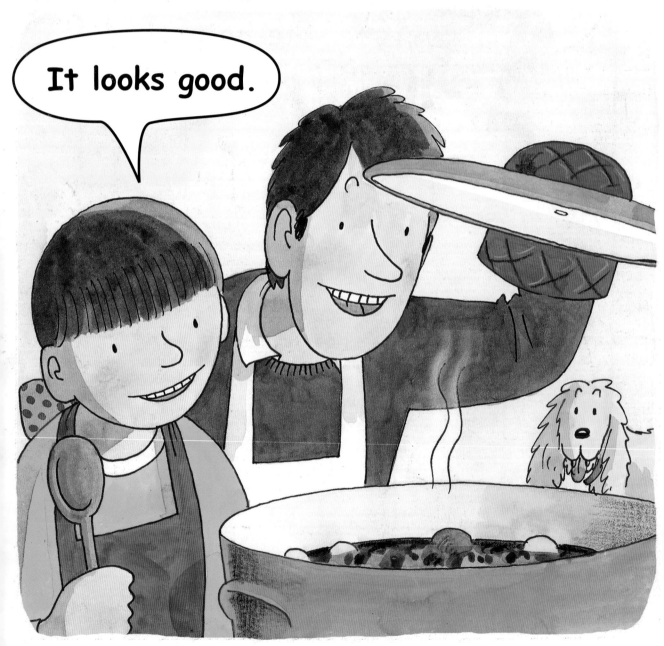

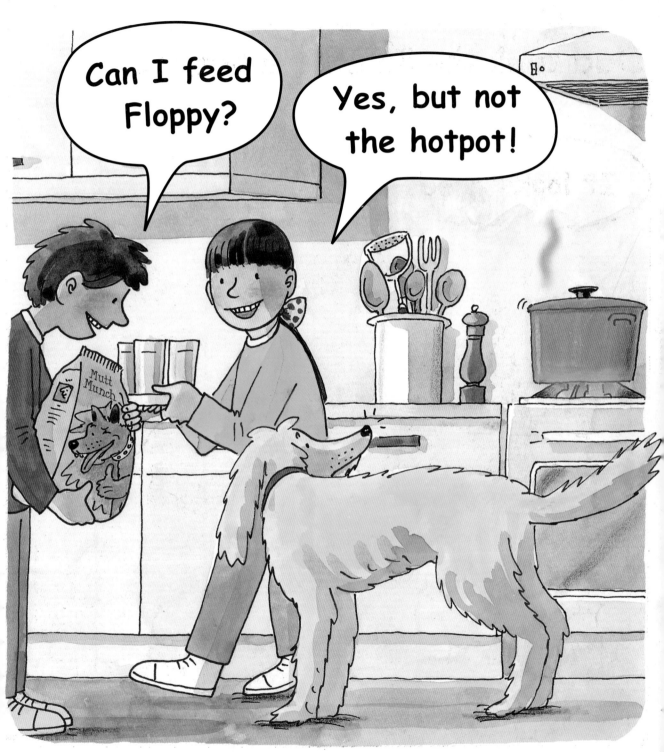

Mum had been to the shop.

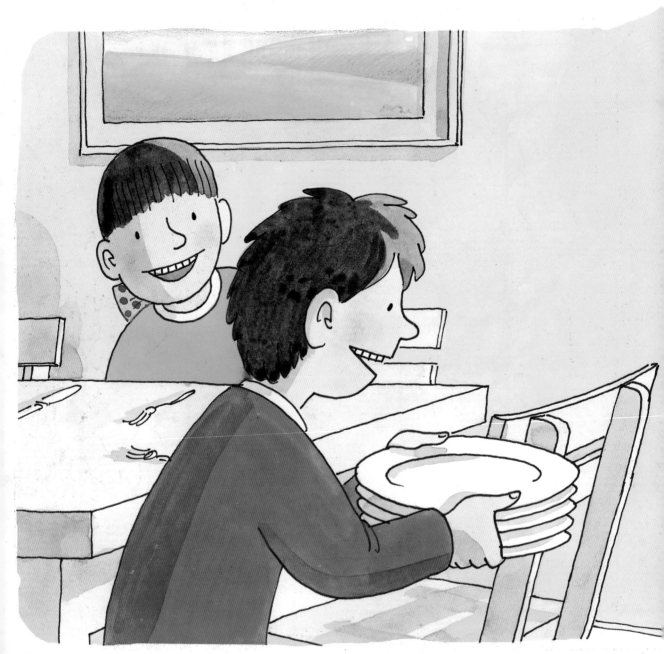

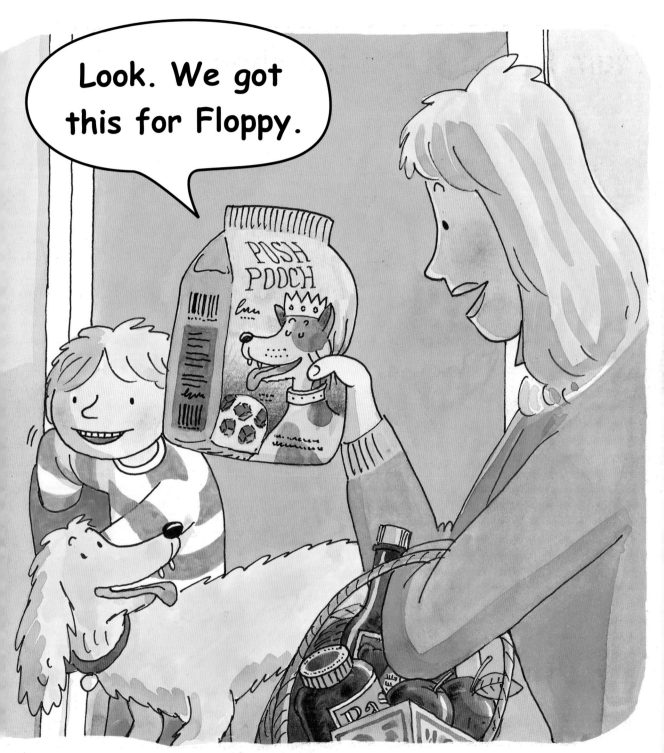

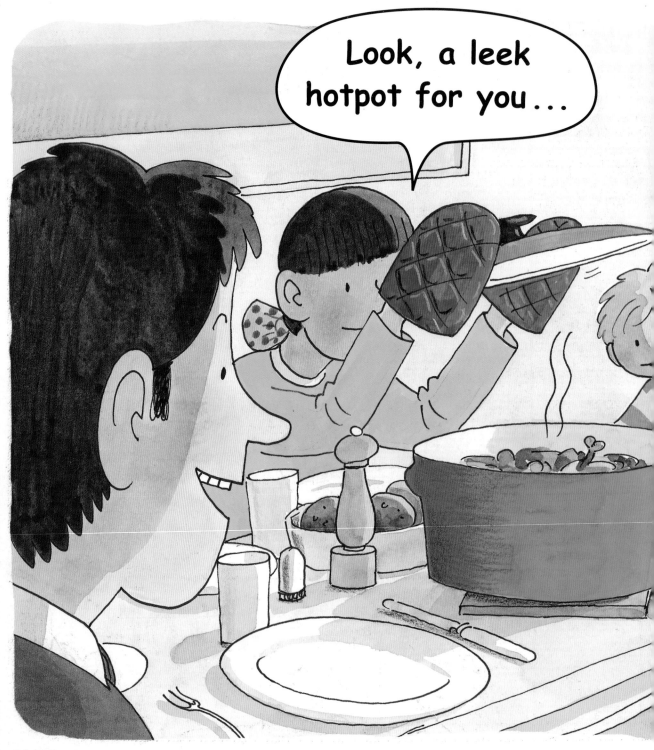

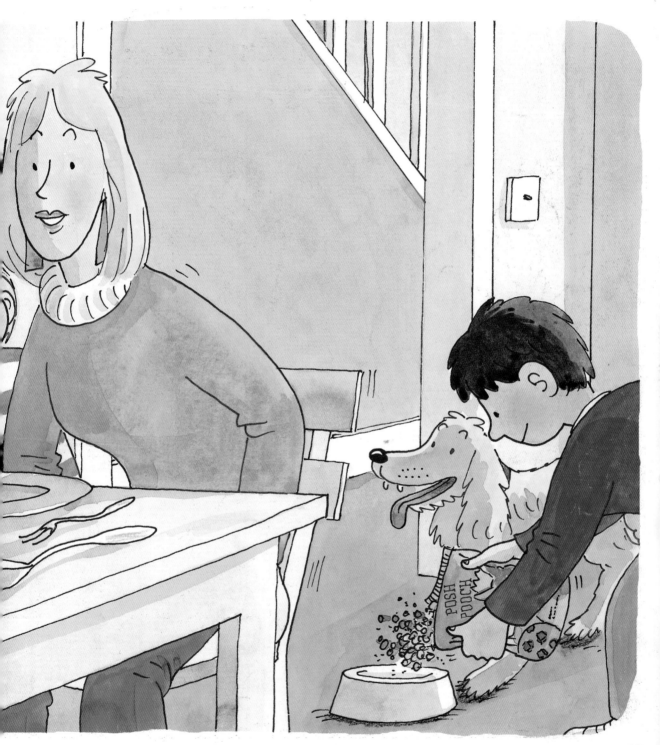

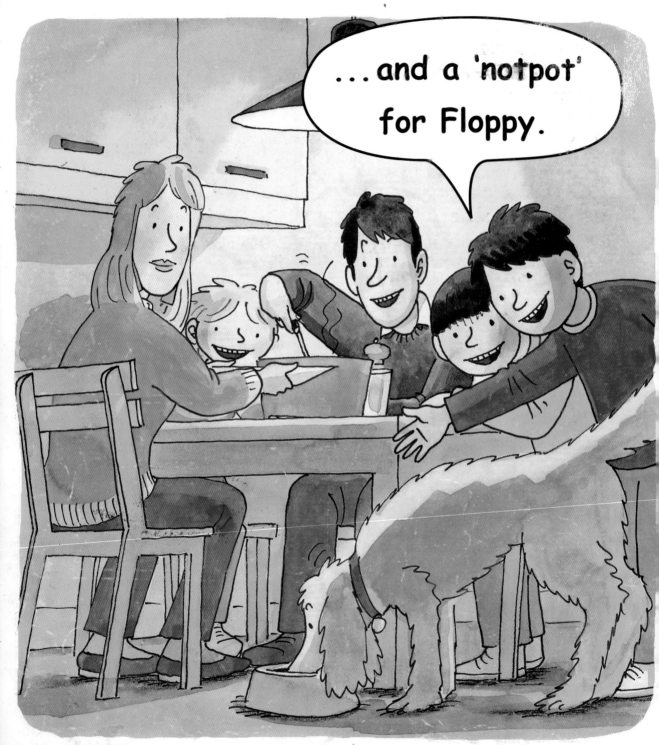